THE ONLINE EARNING BLUEPRINT

A PRACTICAL GUIDE TO BUILDING YOUR INCOME STREAM

ER. TRILOK KUMAR

Made with ♥ on the Notion Press Platform
www.notionpress.com

To all the ambitious individuals who strive to build a better life for themselves and their loved ones. To those who are willing to put in the work, learn new skills, and take calculated risks to achieve their goals.

This book is dedicated to you - the online entrepreneurs, the freelancers, the side hustlers, and the aspiring business owners who are determined to create a successful and sustainable online income stream.

May "The Online Earning Blueprint" be your guide and companion on your journey to online earning success.

My deepest gratitude to all those who supported and encouraged me throughout this process. To my family and friends, thank you for always cheering me on and believing in me. To my colleagues and mentors, thank you for your guidance and inspiration.

May this book be a valuable resource and guide as you embark on your online earning journey, and may you find success and fulfillment along the way.

MUMMY PAPA

Contents

Contents

FOREWORD

The internet has opened up many opportunities for people to earn money online, but it can be difficult to know where to start. "The Online Earning Blueprint" is a book that offers practical advice and expert insights to help readers build a successful online income stream.

This book covers a range of online earning methods such as advertising, affiliate marketing, digital product creation and e-commerce. It's a comprehensive guide that will help you understand the different ways to earn money online and build your income stream in a sustainable and effective way.

I highly recommend this book to anyone looking to start their online earning journey. It provides a clear roadmap to help you achieve your goals and turn your dreams of online earning into a reality.

Preface

The internet has opened up many opportunities for people to earn money online, but it can be difficult to know where to start. "The Online Earning Blueprint" is a book that offers practical advice and expert insights to help readers build a successful online income stream.

This book covers a range of online earning methods such as advertising, affiliate marketing, digital product creation and e-commerce. It's a comprehensive guide that will help you understand the different ways to earn money online and build your income stream in a sustainable and effective way.

I highly recommend this book to anyone looking to start their online earning journey. It provides a clear roadmap to help you achieve your goals and turn your dreams of online earning into a reality.

ACKNOWLEDGEMENTS

From Er. Trilok Kumar,

Writing a book is not a solitary endeavor, and we would like to express our gratitude to those who have helped us in the process of creating "The Online Earning Blueprint."

Firstly, we would like to thank our families for their unwavering support and understanding throughout the writing process. We could not have completed this book without their encouragement and patience.

We also want to express our appreciation to the experts in the field of online earning who have contributed to this book. Your insights and expertise have made this book a valuable resource for anyone looking to build their online earning potential.

Finally, we want to thank our publisher and the entire team who have worked tirelessly to bring this book to fruition. Your dedication and hard work have made this book a reality, and we are grateful for your support.

To all those who have contributed to this book, we extend our heartfelt gratitude. This book would not be possible without your contributions, and we are honored to have worked with each and every one of you.

PROLOGUE

The world has changed, and the way we earn money has changed with it. The internet has opened up new opportunities for people to make money from the comfort of their homes.

"The Online Earning Blueprint" is a book that provides practical advice and expert insights on how to build a successful and sustainable online income stream. We understand that there are many options available when it comes to earning money online, and it can be challenging to know where to start.

In this book, we aim to provide you with a comprehensive guide to help you understand the different ways to earn money online, and how to build your online presence to maximize your earning potential. From advertising and affiliate marketing to digital product creation and e-commerce, we cover a wide range of online earning methods.

Our goal is to help you take the first steps towards achieving your online earning goals. Whether you're just starting out, or looking to take your online earning to the next level, "The Online Earning Blueprint" is a book that can help you achieve your goals.

So, let's get started on this journey of online earning success!

About Author

Er. Trilok Kumar ,

Some if his Achievement award/nomination if any.

एक भारतीय

His name has been Recommended for Honorary Doctorate from World Record University for his Extraordinary Achievement.

-Certified Writer (Poet)

-[Shortlisted for the Top 100 prodigies from across the World]

-[selected as a delegate of the Asia World Model United Nations Virtual Conference, 27-29 August 2021]

-Official Participant of 'GWR' , 'MBR', 'WBR

-[Name has been Approved for NCA 100 Rising Author and Educationist]

-Earned a badge from CertiProf ?

-[Selected for India Prime Top 100 Author and Recharchers 2022]

-[Selected for Harvard-Youth Change the World Workshop - 100 students who come from 6 different countries, 37 cities and 43 schools]

-[selected to join the Future Leaders

Model United Nations, to be held from 4th to 7th March 2022 in Istanbul, Turkey]

-Co author of -

Euphoria

Dreams

Wanderlust

Mind Maze

Royal

Poem and Short Stories

-[Selected for International Social Hounerable Award]

-Nominated for Global Citizen Prize: Cisco Youth Leadership Award

-i have been selected among 5422 applicants as one of the delegate of Arab Youth International MUN 2022.

-shortlisted for BE STAR AWARDS.

-Selected as an eminent personality for 100 powerful personalities 2022 by Glantor X Media.

-Achieved 250 e certificate during lockdown period.

-selected for The Leading Attainers Award 2022, organized by JEC Publication.

Shortlisted for Be Star Award 2022

-Congratulations Trilok Kumar for making it to the Literary Awards 2022!! -Young Adult Author of the Year

-Selected for Bharat Bhushan Award 2022

-Mr. Trilok Kumar has been selected as the delegate of Istanbul International

-Model United Nations which is to be held at Istanbul

-National Book of Records Approved .

-India Book of Record Holder.

-nomination is approved for India Top 100 Educators 2022

-Being recommended for an Honorary doctorate by the India Book of Records for my extraordinary achievements!

Trilok Kumar

"राष्ट्रीय *रत्न* *सम्मान*- *2022"*

-Youngest Writer-

-Selected in Harvard Youth YLC Conference 2023.

About Author

trilok

Introducing Trilok Kumar, a certified writer and poet who has been shortlisted for the Top 100 prodigies from across the world. His achievements include being selected as a delegate of the Asia World Model United Nations Virtual Conference, an official participant of 'GWR', 'MBR', and 'WBR', and earning a badge from CertiProf.

Trilok is also a co-author of several books, including Euphoria, Dreams, Wanderlust, Mind Maze, Royal, Poem and Short Stories. His talent as a writer has been recognized by many, including being selected for the India Prime Top 100 Author and Researchers 2022, the Literary Awards 2022 (Young Adult Author of the Year), and the Bharat Bhushan Award 2022.

In addition, Trilok is an accomplished educator, having been nominated for the India Top 100 Educators 2022. He has also achieved 250+ e-certificates during the lockdown period, demonstrating his dedication to learning and personal growth.

Trilok has been selected for various international events, including the Harvard-Youth Change the World Workshop, the Future Leaders Model United Nations in Istanbul, and the Arab Youth International MUN 2022. He has also been selected as an eminent personality for 100 powerful personalities 2022 by Glantor X Media and shortlisted for the Be Star Award 2022.

His remarkable achievements have earned him the National Book of Records Approval and the India Book of Record Holder title. Trilok has been recommended for an Honorary doctorate degree by the India Book of Records for his extraordinary achievements, and has been awarded the राष्ट्रीय रत्न सम्मान- 2022 as the Youngest Writer.

Trilok's incredible journey and achievements are truly inspiring, making him an exceptional role model for aspiring writers and educators. His works are an inspiration for many, and his dedication to excellence continues to inspire others to pursue their dreams with passion and hard work.

I

Understanding Online Earning

The first step in building your online income stream is to understand what it is and how it works. Online earning refers to any form of income that you generate through the internet.

The internet has opened up new opportunities for people to earn money online. In this chapter, we will cover the basics of online earning and how it works, the advantages and challenges of earning money online, and common myths and misconceptions about online earning.

The beauty of online earning is that it provides you with the freedom to work from anywhere in the world, and on your own schedule. Whether you're a freelancer or an entrepreneur, online earning can be a great way to build financial independence and create a lifestyle that suits you.

Section 1: The basics of online earning and how it works

Online earning refers to making money through the internet. It involves creating and promoting products or services online, generating revenue through online advertising or affiliate marketing, or offering online consultation and services.

There are several types of businesses that can be started online, such as:

E-commerce stores: selling physical or digital products online

Dropshipping: selling products without keeping inventory by partnering with wholesalers

Online services: offering consulting services or digital services such as design, writing, programming, or social media management

Affiliate marketing: promoting other companies' products or services and earning commissions for sales

Online advertising: selling advertising space on your website or social media accounts

Online courses: creating and selling educational content and courses

There are various business models that can be used for online earning, including:

Selling products: creating or sourcing products to sell online, such as through an e-commerce store or a dropshipping business

Offering services: providing online services such as consulting, writing, or programming

Affiliate marketing: promoting other companies' products or services and earning commissions on sales

Advertising: selling ad space on your website or social media accounts

Subscription-based models: charging a recurring fee for access to premium content, services, or products

To start earning online, you will need certain basic technology and tools such as:

A website or blog: to establish your online presence and showcase your products or services

A payment processor: to accept payments online securely

A computer or mobile device: to manage your business online and communicate with clients or customers

Internet access: to maintain your online presence, communicate with customers, and handle transactions

By understanding the basics of online earning, including the different types of businesses and business models, as well as the technology and tools required, you can begin to explore the many opportunities available for earning money online.

In this chapter, we'll explore the different ways to earn money online, including:

Freelancing: Freelancing is a great way to earn money online, especially if you have skills such as writing, graphic design, or programming. Freelancing involves offering your services to clients on a project-by-project basis.

Affiliate Marketing: Affiliate marketing is a process where you earn a commission by promoting other people's products or services. You can promote products through your blog or social media, and earn a commission on each sale that is made through your unique affiliate link.

Advertising: If you have a website or a blog, you can earn money through advertising. Advertising can take the form of banner ads, text ads, or sponsored posts.

Digital Product Creation: Creating and selling digital products such as e-books, online courses, or software can be a lucrative way to earn money online.

E-Commerce: E-commerce involves selling physical products online. This can be done through platforms such as Amazon, Etsy, or your own website.

Online advertising: Online advertising refers to the use of internet-based platforms to promote a business or product. This can include search engine marketing, social media advertising, and display advertising.

Monetization: Monetization refers to the process of making money from an online platform or website. This can be done through various methods, such as advertising, selling products or services, or affiliate marketing.

Section 2: Advantages and challenges of earning money online

Earning money online has many advantages, but also presents unique challenges. In this section, we will explore both the advantages and challenges of earning money online.

Advantages of earning money online:

Flexibility: One of the most significant advantages of earning money online is the flexibility it offers. You can work from home or anywhere with an internet connection and set your own hours. This flexibility allows you to balance work and other life priorities, such as family, hobbies, or travel.

Low startup costs: Starting an online business typically requires lower initial investment compared to traditional brick-and-mortar businesses. You don't need a physical storefront or inventory, which saves you significant costs.

Potential for passive income: Online businesses can generate passive income, which means you can make money even when you are not actively working. For instance, you can earn passive income through affiliate marketing, advertising, or online courses.

Challenges of earning money online:

Need for self-discipline: Working from home requires strong self-discipline and the ability to manage your time effectively. Without the structure of a traditional workplace, it's easy to get distracted and lose focus. It's essential to set clear goals, establish a routine, and avoid distractions to be productive.

Potential for scams and fraud: Online earning also presents risks of scams and fraud. It's essential to be cautious of offers that seem too good to be true and conduct thorough research before investing your time and money into any opportunity. Scammers often prey on people's desperation to earn money quickly or promise large profits for little effort.

By understanding both the advantages and challenges of earning money online, you can make an informed decision about whether online earning is the right fit for you. While online earning presents unique challenges, the potential for flexibility, low startup costs, and passive income make it an attractive opportunity for many.

Section 3: Common myths and misconceptions about online earning

There are many common myths and misconceptions about online earning that can lead people to have unrealistic expectations about the process. In this section, we will explore some of these myths and explain why they are not accurate.

Myth #1: Online earning is easy, and you can get rich quickly Reality: Online earning, like any other form of business, requires hard work, persistence, and patience. While the internet has opened up many opportunities for earning money online, there is no magic formula that can make you rich quickly. It takes time, effort, and a willingness to learn and adapt to new challenges.

Myth #2: You don't need any skills or expertise to earn money online Reality: To succeed in earning money online, you need to have some skills and expertise in your chosen field. Whether you are offering services, creating digital products, or promoting other companies' products, you need to have a strong understanding of your niche and the ability to deliver high-quality products or services.

Myth #3: Online earning is only for young people or tech-savvy individuals Reality: Anyone can earn money online, regardless of age or technical skills. While it's true that technology plays a significant role in online earning, there are many tools and resources available that can help even those with limited technical skills succeed online.

Myth #4: You can make money online without any investment Reality: While it's true that online earning requires lower initial investment compared to traditional businesses, it still requires some investment, whether it's in the form of time or money. To build a successful online business, you need to invest in your website, marketing, and other tools and resources that can help you grow your business.

By understanding the common myths and misconceptions about online earning and the realities of the process, you can approach online earning with a realistic mindset. Hard work, persistence, and patience are key to building a successful online business, but with the right mindset and approach, earning money online can be a fulfilling and rewarding experience.

In this chapter, we've covered the basics of online earning, and introduced you to the different ways to make money online. The key to success is to find the method that works best for you, and then focus on building your online presence to maximize your earning potential.

II

Finding Your Niche

To be successful in online earning, it's important to find your niche. A niche is a specific area of interest or expertise that you can focus on and use to attract a target audience.

Finding your niche is the foundation of building a successful online presence. It's important to choose a niche that you're passionate about, and that has a high demand in the market.

or,

Finding the right niche is essential to building a successful online business. In this chapter, we will explore the importance of finding your niche and the process of identifying the right one for you.

Understanding the importance of finding your niche

Your niche is your unique area of expertise and interest within a larger market. It's the specific group of people or the particular problem you are trying to solve with your products or services. Finding the right niche is critical for several reasons:

You can establish yourself as an expert in your niche and build a loyal customer base

Focusing on a specific niche makes it easier to market and promote your business to the right audience

By catering to a particular niche, you can differentiate yourself from competitors and offer unique value to your customers.

Identifying gaps in the market and opportunities for innovation

To stand out in a crowded market, you need to identify gaps in the market and opportunities for innovation. Here are some tips:

Identify unmet needs: Look for gaps in the market where customers' needs are not being met. This can be an opportunity to create products or services that solve these unmet needs.

Find new angles: Consider ways to differentiate yourself from competitors by offering unique features, services, or a different angle on an existing product or service.

Conduct customer research: Conduct surveys, interviews, or focus groups to gain insights into what customers want and need. This can help you identify opportunities for innovation and improvement.

In this chapter, we'll explore how to find your niche by following these simple steps:

Identify Your Interests: Start by identifying your interests and areas of expertise. What are you passionate about? What topics do you have a lot of knowledge in? Your niche should be something you enjoy and can talk about for hours on end.

Research the Market: Once you've identified your interests, research the market to see if there is a demand for your niche. Look for keywords related to your niche and use tools like Google Trends or SEMrush to see if people are searching for it.

Analyze Your Competition: It's also important to analyze your competition to see what they're doing, and how you can differentiate yourself. Look at their websites, social media, and content to see what's working for them.

Define Your Target Audience: Defining your target audience is critical in finding your niche. Who are you trying to reach? What are their interests and needs? Understanding your target audience will help you create content that resonates with them.

Assess your skills and expertise: Consider your skills, knowledge, and expertise. You can build a niche around your skills and experience.

Test your niche: Test your niche by creating a minimum viable product (MVP) or offering a service on a small scale. This will help you gauge the demand and viability of your niche before investing too much time or resources.

Evaluate the competition: Look at the competition in each niche you're considering. Consider factors such as the number of competitors, the quality of their products or services, and the demand for their offerings.

By finding your niche, you'll be able to create a targeted strategy that will help you stand out in a crowded market and build a loyal following. With these simple steps, you can find your niche and start your journey towards online earning success.

III

Creating a Plan for Online Earning

Now that you've found your niche, it's time to create a plan for online earning. Having a plan will help you stay organized, focused, and motivated towards achieving your goals.

In this chapter, we will discuss the importance of developing a strategic plan for your online earning and the steps to create a roadmap to achieve your goals.

Developing a strategic plan for online earning

A strategic plan is a roadmap that outlines your vision, mission, and goals for your online business. It helps you focus on what you want to achieve and how you plan to achieve it. Here are some steps to follow when developing a strategic plan:

Define your mission and vision: Your mission statement outlines your purpose for starting the business, while your vision statement explains what you hope to achieve in the future.

Conduct a SWOT analysis: SWOT analysis helps you identify your business's strengths, weaknesses, opportunities, and threats. It enables you to leverage your strengths and opportunities while minimizing your weaknesses and threats.

Define your target audience: Identify your target audience by developing buyer personas. These personas represent your ideal customer and help you create products and services that meet their needs.

Develop a value proposition: Your value proposition defines the unique value you offer to your customers. It helps you stand out from the competition and communicate your strengths to potential customers.

In this chapter, we'll explore how to create a plan for online earning by following these simple steps:

Set Your Goals: Start by setting your goals. What do you want to achieve with your online presence? Are you looking to make a full-time income, or just some extra cash? Define your goals and set a timeline for achieving them.

Choose Your Platforms: Next, you'll need to choose the platforms you'll use to monetize your niche. Will you create a blog, YouTube channel, or social media accounts? Each platform has its own benefits and drawbacks, so choose the one that aligns with your goals and target audience.

Develop Your Content Strategy: Once you've chosen your platforms, it's time to develop a content strategy. What type of content will you create? How often will you post? Your content should be informative, engaging, and aligned with your niche and target audience.

Implement Monetization Strategies: Finally, it's time to implement monetization strategies. There are many ways to monetize your online presence, including affiliate marketing, sponsorships, and advertising. Choose the strategies that align with your goals and target audience.

Define your income goals: Determine how much money you want to make and set specific, measurable goals for your online business.

Identify your target audience: Knowing your target audience is essential to creating products, services, and content that they will be interested in.

Choose a niche: Focus on a specific area of expertise to differentiate yourself from competitors and establish yourself as an authority in your field.

Research your market: Conduct research to identify opportunities and gaps in your market that you can fill with your products or services.

Develop a product or service: Based on your research and expertise, create a product or service that addresses the needs of your target audience.

Develop a marketing plan: Determine the best channels to promote your product or service, such as social media, email marketing, or paid advertising.

Set up a sales funnel: Create a sales funnel that guides potential customers through the buying process, from awareness to purchase.

Evaluate and adjust your plan: Regularly track your progress and adjust your plan as needed to ensure that you are meeting your income goals.

Creating a timeline and roadmap for achieving your goals

To achieve your objectives, you need to create a timeline and roadmap that outlines the tasks and activities you need to complete to achieve your goals. Here are some steps to follow:

Break down your goals into smaller milestones: Break down your objectives into smaller milestones that are easier to achieve. For example, if your objective is to increase website traffic by 50%, you can break it down into smaller milestones, such as increasing traffic by 10% each month.

Assign responsibilities and deadlines: Assign responsibilities and deadlines to each milestone. This helps ensure that everyone on your team understands what they need to do and when they need to do it.

Monitor progress and adjust your plan: Monitor your progress towards achieving your goals regularly. If you are not on track to achieving your objectives, adjust your plan and make the necessary changes.

By following these simple steps, you can create a plan for online earning that will help you achieve your goals and build a successful online presence. Remember to stay consistent, focused, and open to learning as you navigate the world of online earning.

IV

Building Your Online Presence

Now that you have a plan for online earning, it's time to start building your online presence. In this chapter, we'll explore the steps you can take to build a strong and effective online presence.

Build Your Website: A website is the foundation of your online presence. It's the place where your audience can find all of your content and learn more about your niche. Building a website doesn't have to be difficult. You can use platforms like WordPress or Wix to create a professional-looking website quickly and easily.

Create Content: Your online presence will only be effective if you create quality content that engages and informs your audience. Content can take many forms, including blog posts, videos, social media updates, and more. The key is to create content that is relevant to your niche and audience.

Promote Your Content: Once you've created your content, it's important to promote it so that your audience can find it. There are many ways to promote your content, including social media, email marketing, and paid advertising. Choose the strategies that align with your goals and target audience.

Engage with Your Audience: Finally, it's important to engage with your audience. Respond to comments and messages, ask for feedback, and create opportunities for your audience to interact with you. Building a strong relationship with your audience will help you to build a loyal following and increase your online earning potential.

Create a website or blog: This will be the foundation of your online presence. Your website or blog should reflect your brand and provide valuable content to your audience.

Develop a content strategy: Consistently creating and sharing high-quality content is essential to building your online presence. This can include blog posts, videos, podcasts, or social media posts.

Establish a social media presence: Social media is a powerful tool for building your brand and connecting with your audience. Choose the social media platforms that are most relevant to your niche and create engaging content.

Build an email list: Email marketing is an effective way to connect with your audience and promote your products or services. Offer incentives such as a free ebook or discount code to encourage people to subscribe to your email list.

Use search engine optimization (SEO): Optimizing your website and content for search engines can help your website rank higher in search results and attract more organic traffic.

Engage with your audience: Respond to comments and messages, ask for feedback, and encourage engagement with your content.

By implementing these strategies, you can build a strong online presence and establish yourself as an authority in your niche. This will help you attract and retain an audience, which is key to making money online.

By following these steps, you can build a strong and effective online presence that will help you to achieve your online earning goals. Remember to stay consistent, create quality content, and engage with your audience.

V

Monetizing Your Online Presence

Now that you have a plan and a strong online presence, it's time to start monetizing your efforts. In this chapter, we'll explore the different ways you can monetize your online presence and start earning money.

Affiliate Marketing: One of the most popular ways to monetize your online presence is through affiliate marketing. This involves promoting other people's products and earning a commission for any sales made through your unique affiliate link. You can find affiliate programs in your niche by searching online or by contacting companies directly.

Sponsored Content: You can also earn money by creating sponsored content. This involves working with brands to create content that promotes their products or services. In exchange, you'll receive payment or other perks, such as free products or exposure to a new audience.

Advertising: Another way to monetize your online presence is through advertising. You can place ads on your website or social media channels and earn money when your audience clicks on them or views them. There are many advertising networks available, such as Google AdSense and MediaVine, that can help you monetize your content.

Online Courses and Products: If you have expertise in a particular area, you can create and sell online courses or products. These can include eBooks, webinars, and online courses that teach your audience valuable skills or information. This can be a lucrative way to monetize your online presence, as you can earn money from your expertise and knowledge.

Freelance Work: Finally, you can monetize your online presence by offering your services as a freelancer. This can include writing, design, consulting, and more. You can use your online presence to showcase your skills and attract new clients.

E-commerce: Sell your own products or services on your website or social media platforms. Platforms like Shopify or WooCommerce can help you set up an online store.

Online courses or digital products: Create and sell online courses or digital products such as ebooks, printables, or templates.

Subscription-based model: Offer premium content or services to your audience through a subscription-based model. Patreon is a popular platform for creators to monetize their content through monthly subscriptions.

Consulting or coaching: Offer your expertise in a specific niche through consulting or coaching services.

When it comes to monetizing your online presence, it's important to choose methods that align with your values and your audience's needs. Be transparent about any paid content or promotions and prioritize building trust and relationships with your audience. Remember that it takes time and effort to build a successful online presence, so be patient and stay committed to providing value to your audience.

By exploring these different monetization strategies, you can start earning money from your online presence. Remember to choose strategies that align with your goals and target audience, and to stay consistent in your efforts. With persistence and hard work, you can turn your online presence into a profitable venture.

VI
Scaling Your Online Business

Once you have established your online presence and started earning money, it's time to focus on scaling your online business. In this chapter, we'll discuss the different ways you can grow your business and take it to the next level.

Expand Your Product or Service Offerings: One way to scale your online business is to expand your product or service offerings. You can add new products or services that are related to your existing offerings, or you can target a new audience with a new set of products or services.

Create a Sales Funnel: A sales funnel is a series of steps that a potential customer goes through before making a purchase. By creating a sales funnel, you can guide your audience towards making a purchase and increase your conversion rate.

Automate Your Business Processes: Automating your business processes can help you save time and scale your business more efficiently. You can automate tasks such as email marketing, social media scheduling, and customer service.

Outsource Tasks: Outsourcing tasks can help you free up your time and focus on growing your business. You can outsource tasks such as content creation, customer service, and website design to experts in those areas.

Collaborate with Others: Collaboration can help you reach new audiences and grow your business more quickly. You can collaborate with other businesses in your niche or partner with influencers to promote your products or services.

By focusing on these strategies, you can scale your online business and reach new levels of success. Remember to track your progress and adjust your strategy as needed. With dedication and hard work, you can take your online business to the next level. or some other statergies are also follows,

Expand your product line: Once you have established a successful product, consider expanding your offerings to include related products or services. This can help you reach a wider audience and increase your revenue.

Paid advertising: Utilizing paid advertising, such as Facebook or Google ads, can help you reach a larger audience and increase your sales.

Outsourcing and hiring: Consider outsourcing or hiring employees to help with tasks that are time-consuming or outside of your expertise. This can help you focus on more important tasks and free up your time.

Automate your systems: Implementing systems such as email automation or website chatbots can help automate processes and save time.

Collaborate with other businesses: Partnering with other businesses in your niche can help you reach a wider audience and potentially bring in new customers.

Diversify your income streams: Consider adding new income streams to your business, such as affiliate marketing or creating a membership site. This can help you generate additional income and reduce your reliance on one income source.

By implementing these strategies, you can scale your online business and reach your income goals without necessarily putting in more effort or time.

VII

Growing Your Online Income

In this chapter, we will explore different strategies for growing your online income. Whether you are a freelancer, blogger, or e-commerce store owner, there are numerous ways to scale your online business and increase your revenue.

Understanding the Online Economy

To grow your online income, it is essential to have a good understanding of the online economy. This includes the different ways that people make money online, such as through e-commerce, online advertising, affiliate marketing, and more. By having a clear understanding of the online economy, you can identify new opportunities for monetizing your online presence and driving more revenue.

Creating a Plan for Growth

To grow your online income, it is important to have a plan in place. This plan should outline your goals, identify the key metrics you will use to measure your progress, and provide a roadmap for achieving your objectives. Some key elements of a growth plan include identifying your target audience, developing a marketing strategy, and setting realistic revenue goals.

Building Your Online Presence

To grow your online income, it is essential to have a strong online presence. This includes having a well-designed website that is optimized for search engines, building a following on social media, and developing a reputation as an expert in your field. By building a strong online presence, you can attract more traffic to your website, generate more leads, and build a loyal customer base.

Monetizing Your Online Presence

To increase your online income, you need to monetize your online presence. There are many ways to do this, such as through advertising, affiliate marketing, selling products or services, and more. The key is to identify the methods that work best for your business and audience, and to continuously test and refine your approach to optimize your revenue.

Scaling Your Online Business

To grow your online income, you need to scale your online business. This means finding ways to increase your revenue while minimizing your expenses. Some strategies for scaling your online business include expanding your product or service offerings, automating your business processes, and outsourcing tasks to free up more of your time.

Business Ideas for Online Earning

There are many different business ideas for online earning, such as starting an e-commerce store, offering online courses or coaching services, building a blog or online community, and more. The key is to identify a niche that you are passionate about and that has the potential to generate revenue. By continuously testing and refining your approach, you can build a successful and profitable online business.

Expand your reach: Consider expanding your reach by selling your products or services on other online marketplaces or partnering with other businesses to reach new customers.

Offer promotions and discounts: Offering promotions and discounts can help you attract new customers and incentivize existing customers to make repeat purchases. Consider offering limited-time discounts, free shipping, or other incentives to boost sales.

Invest in automation: Automation can help you streamline your business operations and increase efficiency. Consider using tools like email marketing automation, chatbots, and e-commerce automation to reduce manual tasks and free up your time to focus on growing your business.

Monitor your financials: Keep a close eye on your financials to ensure you're making a profit and to identify areas for improvement. Use tools like accounting software to track your income and expenses and make informed decisions about where to invest your resources.

In conclusion, growing your online income requires dedication, hard work, and a willingness to adapt to changes in the market and online economy. By following these strategies and continuously testing and refining your approach, you can scale your online business and increase your revenue over time.

VII

Managing Your Online Business

Managing an online business requires a unique set of skills and strategies. Here are some tips to help you manage your online business effectively:

Set clear goals: Establish specific, measurable, achievable, relevant, and time-bound (SMART) goals for your online business. This will help you stay focused and motivated, and will allow you to track your progress over time.

Develop a content strategy: Create a content strategy that aligns with your business goals and target audience. Consistently producing high-quality content is essential for building a loyal following and driving traffic to your website.

Prioritize customer service: Provide excellent customer service by responding to inquiries promptly and addressing any concerns or complaints in a timely and professional manner. Happy customers are more likely to refer others to your business.

Manage your finances: Keep track of your income and expenses, and regularly review your financial statements to ensure that your business is profitable. Consider using accounting software or hiring an accountant to help you manage your finances.

Use analytics: Use website analytics to track visitor behavior and identify areas for improvement. Use this data to make informed decisions about your marketing and content strategies.

Stay up-to-date with trends: Stay current with industry trends and technology advancements that could impact your business. Attend industry events, read industry publications, and engage with other professionals in your field.

Automate where possible: Use tools and software to automate routine tasks such as social media scheduling, email marketing, and customer service inquiries. This will free up your time to focus on more strategic tasks.

Remember that running an online business requires dedication, hard work, and continuous learning. Stay committed to providing value to your customers and always be willing to adapt and evolve as your business grows.

Managing Your Finances

Keeping track of your business finances is critical to the success of your online business.

Make sure to create a budget, track your income and expenses, and plan for taxes.

You can use tools such as spreadsheets, accounting software, or hiring an accountant to manage your finances.

Staying Organized and Productive

Staying organized and productive is essential for managing your online business effectively.

Develop a schedule and prioritize your tasks to make the most of your time.

Use tools such as to-do lists, productivity apps, and project management software to stay organized and productive.

Customer Service and Support

Providing good customer service is crucial for building a successful online business.

Make sure to respond to customer inquiries promptly and professionally, offer refunds or exchanges when necessary, and resolve any issues or complaints quickly and efficiently.

Use tools such as helpdesk software or customer service apps to manage customer support.

Dealing with Competition

Competition in the online world can be fierce, but it can also be an opportunity to improve your business.

Look for ways to differentiate yourself from your competitors by offering unique products or services, providing excellent customer service, and continuously improving your business.

Keep an eye on what your competitors are doing and look for ways to stay ahead of the game.

By following these tips and strategies, you can effectively manage your online business and set yourself up for long-term success.

IX

Overcoming Challenges and Obstacles

The Online Earning Blueprint" is actually about managing your online business, not about overcoming challenges and obstacles. However, here are some key points related to overcoming challenges and obstacles for online entrepreneurs in simple language:

Expect challenges: Building an online business is not easy and there will be challenges and obstacles along the way. Be prepared to face them.

Stay flexible: The online landscape is constantly changing and evolving, so be willing to adapt and change your strategy as needed.

Seek help and support: Don't be afraid to ask for help and support when you need it. Join online communities, network with other entrepreneurs, or hire a business coach or mentor for guidance and support.

Learn from failures: Failures and setbacks are normal when building a business. Use them as opportunities to learn and improve your business.

Stay motivated: Building a successful online business takes time and effort, so it's important to stay motivated and focused on your goals. Celebrate small wins along the way and keep working towards your long-term vision.

<u>Here is 10 points more.</u>

Here are 10 key points about overcoming challenges and obstacles for online entrepreneurs:

Building an online business is not easy, and challenges and obstacles are inevitable.

Be flexible and adaptable, as the online landscape is constantly changing.

Seek help and support from others, including online communities, networking, and business coaches/mentors.

Failure and setbacks are normal, so use them as opportunities to learn and improve.

Stay motivated and focused on your long-term vision for your business.

Maintain a positive attitude and mindset to overcome challenges.

Keep your goals and objectives in mind, and use them as motivation to keep going.

Take breaks and practice self-care to avoid burnout and fatigue.

Be willing to pivot or change your strategy if it's not working.

Celebrate small wins and progress along the way to maintain motivation and momentum.

more to know

Develop a positive mindset: Having a positive mindset can help you see challenges as opportunities for growth and learning, rather than obstacles. Cultivate a positive attitude by practicing gratitude, focusing on your strengths, and finding the silver lining in difficult situations.

Set clear goals: Setting clear goals can help you stay focused and motivated in the face of challenges. Make sure your goals are specific, measurable, achievable, relevant, and time-bound.

Break down the challenge into smaller steps: Breaking down a challenge into smaller, more manageable steps can make it less overwhelming. Focus on one step at a time, and celebrate your progress along the way.

Seek support: Don't be afraid to reach out for help when you're facing a challenge. Seek support from friends, family, or colleagues, or consider working with a coach or therapist who can provide guidance and accountability.

Embrace failure: Failure is a natural part of the learning process. Don't let fear of failure hold you back from taking risks and pursuing your goals. Instead, view failure as an opportunity to learn and grow.

Learn from the experience: After overcoming a challenge, take time to reflect on what you learned from the experience. Use this knowledge to prepare yourself for future challenges and to continue growing and developing.

Remember that challenges and obstacles are a normal part of life. By developing a positive mindset, setting clear goals, seeking support, and learning from your experiences, you can overcome challenges and obstacles and emerge stronger and more resilient.

X

Success Strategies for Online Earning

Success Strategies for Online Earning

- Developing a success mindset
- Learning from successful online earners
- Keeping up with industry trends and developments
- Strategies for long-term success

Developing a success mindset: Success starts with the right mindset. This means being positive, staying motivated, and having a growth mindset that embraces challenges and failures as opportunities for learning and growth.

Learning from successful online earners: One of the best ways to succeed in the online earning world is to learn from those who have already done it. This involves seeking out mentors, attending industry events, reading books and blogs, and taking online courses.

Keeping up with industry trends and developments: The online earning industry is constantly evolving, so it's important to stay up-to-date with the latest trends and developments. This includes reading industry news, following thought leaders on social media, and attending relevant webinars and conferences.

Strategies for long-term success: Long-term success in online earning requires a combination of strategic planning, consistent effort, and a focus on customer satisfaction. This includes setting realistic goals, creating a business plan, developing a strong online presence, offering quality products or services, and prioritizing customer service and support.

Here are some more points we need to understand ,

Success in online earning requires a combination of strategies that enable you to attract and retain customers, create value, and generate revenue. Here are some success strategies for online earning:

Develop a niche: By focusing on a specific niche, you can differentiate yourself from the competition and provide more targeted solutions to your customers' needs.

Offer high-quality products or services: Provide exceptional value to your customers by offering products or services that are unique, high-quality, and solve a specific problem or need.

Build trust and credibility: Establish trust and credibility with your customers by being transparent, honest, and delivering on your promises. Provide customer testimonials, social proof, and customer support to demonstrate that you are committed to providing the best customer experience.

Create a strong brand identity: A strong brand identity can help you stand out from the competition and create a loyal following. Develop a consistent brand image, including a logo, colors, and messaging, that resonates with your target audience.

Utilize social media: Social media is a powerful tool for building your online presence and connecting with your customers. Use social media platforms to promote your products or services, engage with your audience, and drive traffic to your website.

Offer excellent customer service: Customer service is crucial for building customer loyalty and repeat business. Respond to customer inquiries promptly, provide exceptional support, and go above and beyond to exceed their expectations.

Continuously evaluate and improve: Continuously evaluate and improve your online earning strategies by analyzing data, monitoring customer feedback, and identifying areas for improvement. Implement changes to optimize your business and maximize your revenue.

XI

Final Thoughts

Accourding to me you are going to utilize any of the above tricks the one things is necessary in all the cases is the Mindset, a powerful and balanced mindset is very important ,

taking the example of our examination system now a day student are only studying ofr the purpose of passing the exam not for their excellence ofcourse they have northing to do with all these things, but this things is not applicable for always with everyone.

Therec is a little bit difference between Lucl and Achievement,

IF YOU GOT SUCCEED WITH NEFGATIVE ATTITUDE IT IS CALLED LUCK,
BUT AT A TIME WHEN YOU GOT SUCEED IN LIFE WITH POSITIVE ATTITUDE IT IS CALLED ACHEVEMENT.

So the point is that here who worked hard for their task and for their goal ofcourse they got suceed but the same time who didnt worked hard sometimes they also gettingg the same , as many of the people observing that things and makes a example that he didnt worked hard and after then also he got success, burt they forgot at that that that was just a luck.

SDo coming to The Topic again wheathere you want to do b;loggin, freelancing, youtube channel, selling digital products or affiliate marketing etc. any of them tyou want to do that required a Full consistency, a poerful mindset and powerful thinking. Try to bee see the big Dream , if i gonna tell me about myself ,

when i was in 5th semester of my engineering there was the time of Corona all the people looking for a job to generate extra income , i was also from that i also try to join some place for earning money so i start searching all about the whole google , but i put one condition that i have no resources, SO, during that period i actually attended approx 50 + webinar online from differnt sources from very bigger companies like i have attended the webinar of Bada Businnes , I have first time i have attened the business Webinar of Bada Business. Then also attended the webinar of Vestige, Forever Living product, also attened the Various meeting of Various Business Models Iwas completely involves in that process but i have told you earlier that i having one thought that i didnt having any resources so i was basically searching for free , but i got nothing .

Soon i got idea that how they work first they will contact you once you will fill any form from any source then they will contact you and ask you for simple information like name email etc. then tehy eill tell you to attend a webinar as we have recuieved many application like you so attend that webinar and ofcourse you will get the information about the company , firstly they will not revel the name of the company in the webinar they gonna revel the name of the company , Then you gonna understand that if you want to join then you have to pay some amount .

So this types of things i will understood during this period.And ofcourse it is ok that

while i gonna take the example of You tube will get video on each and every topic but no one taking serously so they gonna apply the tacknik of IF YOU PAY YOU PAY ATTENTION its true.

In conclusion, online earning provides a vast range of opportunities for entrepreneurs to start and grow their businesses in the digital age. However, to achieve success, it's important to have a clear understanding of the basics of online earning and the challenges and advantages that come with it. Finding your niche, creating a strategic plan, and building a strong online presence are critical for success in online earning. Additionally, developing a strong brand identity, offering high-quality products or services, and providing exceptional customer service can help you build trust and credibility with your customers and increase your revenue.

Remember, success in online earning requires patience, persistence, and hard work. It's essential to continuously evaluate and improve your strategies to stay ahead of the competition and adapt to changing market conditions. With the right approach, resources, and mindset, you can achieve success and achieve your goals in the exciting world of online earning.

Common Earning Methods

1. Online surveys and paid focus groups

2. Selling goods or services on online marketplaces like Amazon, eBay, or Etsy

3. Online tutoring or teaching courses

4. Virtual bookkeeping, accounting, or other administrative services

5. Affiliate marketing and promoting other people's products

6. Dropshipping - selling products from a supplier directly to the customer without holding inventory

7. Creating and selling digital products like ebooks, courses, or software

8. Blogging or content creation and earning ad revenue

9. Social media management and marketing services

10. Online coaching or consulting services

Here are also some methods which we consider for earning money along with example are follows,

Advertising revenue: This method involves displaying ads on your website, blog, or social media channels and earning revenue when viewers click on or view the ads.

Google AdSense is a popular platform for earning advertising revenue.

Affiliate marketing: This method involves promoting someone else's products or services on your website, blog, or social media channels and earning a commission on any resulting sales or leads. Amazon Associates is a popular affiliate marketing program.

E-commerce: This method involves selling your own products or services online through an e-commerce platform such as Shopify or WooCommerce. Examples of e-commerce businesses include clothing retailers, artisanal food sellers, or digital product creators.

Sponsored content: This method involves partnering with brands and creating sponsored content such as blog posts, social media posts, or videos in exchange for payment. For example, a food blogger might partner with a kitchen appliance company to create a sponsored post featuring their products.

Online courses: This method involves creating and selling online courses or digital products. Udemy and Skillshare are popular platforms for selling online courses.

Subscription-based model: This method involves offering premium content or services to your audience through a subscription-based model. For example, a fitness instructor might offer access to exclusive workout videos and meal plans for a monthly fee.

Remember that each earning method has its own benefits and challenges. It's important to choose a method that aligns with your skills, interests, and values, and to approach it with patience, persistence, and a focus on providing value to your audience.

XII

Conclusion

Introduction to Online Earning

Online earning provides many opportunities and advantages, but it also has its challenges and requires hard work and dedication.

Success in online earning comes from finding a niche, developing a plan, and leveraging technology and tools.

Understanding online earning is crucial for anyone looking to make money on the internet. It involves various activities such as selling products or services, affiliate marketing, or advertising.

To start earning money online, it is important to have a clear understanding of the different business models that can be used and the tools and technology required.

Some advantages of online earning include the flexibility of working from home, the potential for passive income, and the ability to reach a global audience.

However, there are also challenges to online earning, such as the need for self-discipline and the potential for scams and fraud.

It is important to approach online earning with a realistic mindset, understanding that it takes hard work, persistence, and patience to build a successful online business.

Finding your niche is a crucial step in building a successful online business. Your niche is the specific area of focus that your business will specialize in.

To find your niche, it is important to do market research and evaluate market demand. You can use various tools and resources to do this, such as keyword research and competitor analysis.

It is also important to identify gaps in the market and opportunities for innovation. This can help you find a unique angle for your business that sets you apart from competitors.

Once you have identified your niche, it is important to focus on providing high-quality products or services that meet the needs of your target audience. This can help you build a loyal customer base and establish a strong online presence.

It is important to be flexible and willing to adapt as your business grows and evolves. This can help you stay competitive and continue to meet the changing needs of your target audience.

Here are some key conclusion points for "The Online Earning Blueprint" as a whole:

Online earning is a viable option for individuals who want to earn money from the comfort of their own home. It offers a range of advantages, including flexibility and the potential for passive income.

However, there are also challenges associated with online earning, such as the need for self-discipline and the potential for scams and fraud.

To be successful at online earning, it is important to understand the basics of online business, including the different business models and the technology and tools required.

Finding your niche is a crucial step in building a successful online business. This involves doing market research, evaluating market demand, and identifying gaps in the market.

Developing a strategic plan is also crucial for online earning success. This involves setting goals and objectives, creating a timeline, and establishing a roadmap for achieving your goals.

*There are various strategies and techniques th*at can help you grow your online income, such as building your online presence, diversifying your income streams, and focusing on providing value to your target audience.

It is important to be persistent, patient, and adaptable when pursuing online earning opportunities. Success in online earning requires hard work, dedication, and a willingness to learn and grow.

Overall, "The Online Earning Blueprint" provides a comprehensive guide to earning money online, offering practical tips and strategies for individuals who want to start an online business or supplement their income through online earning opportunities.

XII

How business works

Online business, also known as e-commerce, refers to any business or transaction that takes place on the internet. It involves buying and selling products or services over the internet using a website, social media, or any other online platform. Online businesses can range from small-scale businesses to large multinational corporations.

The working of an online business involves several steps, which are as follows:

Creation of a website: The first step in online business is to create a website. The website should be user-friendly and contain all the necessary information about the products or services that the business offers.

Marketing: The next step is to market the website. This can be done through search engine optimization, social media, email marketing, and other digital marketing techniques. The aim is to drive traffic to the website and increase its visibility.

Sales: Once the website has been marketed successfully, the next step is to generate sales. Customers can make purchases online using credit or debit cards, PayPal, or other payment methods. The website should have a secure payment gateway to ensure the safety of customers' personal and financial information.

Order fulfillment: After the customer has placed an order, the business needs to fulfill the order. This involves packing and shipping the product to the customer. Some businesses may use a dropshipping model where the product is shipped directly from the manufacturer or supplier to the customer.

Customer service: Good customer service is essential for any online business. Customers may have questions about products, shipping, or returns. It's important for the business to provide prompt and helpful customer service to ensure customer satisfaction.

One example of a successful online business is Amazon.com. Amazon started as an online bookstore in 1995 but has since expanded to sell a wide range of products, including electronics, clothing, and groceries. The company has a user-friendly website that offers fast and reliable delivery, and it has an extensive digital marketing strategy that targets customers with personalized recommendations and promotions. Amazon's success is due in part to its focus on customer service, including fast delivery and easy returns.

XIV

Freelancing model

Freelancing is a way of working independently on a project-by-project basis for various clients, instead of being tied to a single employer. As a freelancer, you can offer your services or expertise in a particular field to a wide range of clients, both individuals and businesses, locally or globally.

Here's an example of how freelancing works:

Let's say you are a graphic designer with expertise in creating logos and you offer your services as a freelancer. You can search for clients on various freelance platforms such as Upwork, Freelancer, Fiverr, or even on social media platforms like LinkedIn, Twitter, or Facebook.

Once you find a potential client who requires a new logo for their business, you can submit a proposal with your portfolio and pricing. If the client is interested, they may select you for the project, and you can discuss the project requirements, timeline, and pricing.

Once both parties agree to the terms, you can start working on the project, and communicate with the client to make sure the design is meeting their expectations. After completing the project, you can submit the design to the client, who can then provide feedback or approve the design.

Finally, the client pays you for your services, and you can receive payment through various payment gateways such as PayPal, bank transfer, or other online payment methods.

This is just one example of how freelancing works, and the process may vary depending on the type of project, the industry, and the specific requirements of the client.

XV

How website work for revenue

A website can generate revenue in a number of ways, depending on the business model and the goals of the website owner. Here are some common ways that websites can generate revenue:

E-commerce: A website can be used to sell products or services online. This is often done through an e-commerce platform that allows customers to browse products, add them to a cart, and make a purchase using a credit card or other payment method. Examples of e-commerce websites include Amazon, Etsy, and Zappos.

Advertising: A website can generate revenue by displaying ads from advertisers. This can be done through programs such as Google AdSense or by selling advertising directly to businesses. The revenue generated is typically based on the number of clicks or impressions that the ads receive. Examples of advertising-based websites include news sites like CNN and entertainment sites like Buzzfeed.

Affiliate marketing: A website can generate revenue by promoting products or services from other companies and earning a commission on sales that are generated through the website. This can be done by including affiliate links in articles or product reviews. Examples of affiliate marketing websites include Wirecutter and BestReviews.

Subscriptions: A website can generate revenue by offering access to premium content or services for a fee. Examples of subscription-based websites include The New York Times and Netflix.

Donations: A website can generate revenue by accepting donations from users. This is often used by non-profit organizations and content creators who rely on the support of their fans. Examples of donation-based websites include Wikipedia and Patreon.

Overall, a website can be a powerful tool for generating revenue if it is designed with a clear business model in mind and provides value to its users.

XVI

5 PILLARS OF ONLINE EARNING

The five pillars of online earning are:

Content Creation: Creating valuable content is the foundation of online earning. You can create content in various forms like videos, blog posts, social media posts, podcasts, eBooks, online courses, and more.

Traffic: Generating traffic to your website or online platform is crucial for online earning. You can drive traffic through various channels like search engine optimization, social media marketing, email marketing, paid advertising, and more.

Audience Engagement: Once you have an audience, engaging with them and building a relationship is essential. Engage with your audience through social media, email marketing, comments, and feedback.

Monetization: There are various ways to monetize your online platform, including advertising, sponsored content, affiliate marketing, digital products, and services. Choose the monetization method that aligns with your audience and content.

Analytics: Analyzing your online platform's performance is essential to improve your earnings. Use tools like Google Analytics to track your website's performance, audience behavior, and other relevant data. Analyzing data can help you make informed decisions and improve your online earning potential.

XVII

Earn without investment

There are several ways to earn money online without investing any money upfront. Here are a few examples:

Freelancing: You can offer your skills and services on various freelancing platforms such as Upwork, Fiverr, and Freelancer. You can work as a content writer, graphic designer, virtual assistant, web developer, and many more.

Online surveys: You can take online surveys and get paid for it. There are many websites such as Swagbucks, Survey Junkie, and Vindale Research that pay you for taking surveys.

Online marketplaces: You can sell your products on various online marketplaces such as Amazon, eBay, and Etsy. You can sell products that you no longer need or create products yourself to sell.

Affiliate marketing: You can promote products of other people and earn a commission for every sale that you generate. You can join affiliate programs of companies such as Amazon, ShareASale, and ClickBank.

Online tutoring: You can teach online and get paid for it. There are many websites such as Chegg, TutorMe, and Skooli that offer online tutoring services. You can teach various subjects such as math, science, and languages.

It's important to note that earning money online without investing any money upfront may require a lot of time and effort to build your skills and develop your online presence.

XVIII

SEO

SEO, or Search Engine Optimization, is the process of optimizing a website to rank higher in search engine results pages (SERPs) for specific keywords or phrases. SEO involves both on-page and off-page optimization techniques to improve the quality and quantity of traffic to a website from search engines.

Here's a brief overview of how SEO works:

Keyword Research: Identify the most relevant and high-traffic keywords related to your website or business.

On-Page Optimization: Optimize the website's content, structure, and HTML code to make it more search engine-friendly. This includes optimizing page titles, meta descriptions, header tags, and content.

Off-Page Optimization: Build high-quality backlinks from relevant and authoritative websites to improve the website's authority and reputation. This includes strategies like guest blogging, social media marketing, and influencer outreach.

Technical Optimization: Optimize the website's technical elements like site speed, mobile responsiveness,

URL structure, and site architecture to improve the user experience and search engine crawlability.

Monitoring and Analysis: Continuously monitor and analyze the website's performance, traffic, and rankings to make data-driven decisions to improve the SEO strategy.

By implementing these techniques, SEO can help a website rank higher in SERPs, attract more organic traffic, and increase revenue and conversions.

XIX

Best website to Learn and Earn

There are many websites that can help you earn money and learn new skills online. Here are some of the best websites for both earning and learning:

Udemy: Udemy is an online learning platform that offers courses in a wide variety of subjects. You can take courses to learn new skills, and some of the courses can even help you start your own business.

Fiverr: Fiverr is a website where you can offer your services to people around the world. You can offer services such as writing, graphic design, web development, and more.

Upwork: Upwork is a freelance marketplace where you can find clients who need your services. You can create a profile, apply for jobs, and work with clients directly.

Swagbucks: Swagbucks is a website that rewards you for completing surveys, watching videos, and playing games. You can earn Swagbucks, which can be redeemed for gift cards or cash.

Amazon Mechanical Turk: Amazon Mechanical Turk is a platform where you can complete small tasks in exchange for payment. These tasks can include things like data entry, content moderation, and more.

Coursera: Coursera is an online learning platform that partners with universities and organizations to offer courses in a wide range of subjects. You can take courses for free, or pay to earn a certificate.

LinkedIn Learning: LinkedIn Learning is an online learning platform that offers courses in business, technology, and creative skills. You can take courses to learn new skills, and some of the courses can even help you advance in your career.

YouTube: YouTube is a video sharing platform where you can find educational videos on almost any topic. You can learn new skills, watch tutorials, and even start your own channel to earn money.

XX

Website for earning Free

There are many websites where you can earn money online for free. Some popular ones include:

Swagbucks - This website pays you to take surveys, watch videos, play games, and shop online.

InboxDollars - InboxDollars pays you to take surveys, watch videos, and read emails.

Survey Junkie - This website pays you to take surveys on a variety of topics.

Amazon Mechanical Turk - This website allows you to complete small tasks for pay, such as data entry or transcription.

Fiverr - Fiverr is a platform where you can offer your services to others, such as graphic design or content writing.

Upwork - Upwork is a freelance platform where you can offer your skills to clients for pay.

UserTesting - UserTesting pays you to test websites and apps and provide feedback on your experience.

It's important to note that while these websites can provide opportunities for earning money online, they may not be a reliable or consistent source of income. It's always a good idea to research and verify the legitimacy of any website before using it to earn money.

XXI

Tools for Online Earning

There are various tools available that can help you in your online earning journey. Here are a few examples:

Google Analytics: This tool helps you analyze your website traffic and user behavior. It provides insights on the number of visitors, page views, bounce rate, and more. With this information, you can make data-driven decisions to improve your website's performance and increase revenue.

Social media platforms: Social media platforms such as Facebook, Instagram, and Twitter provide a great opportunity to connect with potential customers. By building a strong social media presence and sharing valuable content, you can drive traffic to your website and increase your online earning potential.

Email marketing software: Email marketing software such as Mailchimp and Constant Contact can help you create and send email campaigns to your subscribers. By providing valuable content and promotional offers, you can convert subscribers into paying customers.

Online marketplaces: Online marketplaces such as Amazon, eBay, and Etsy provide a platform for selling products online. You can set up your own online store and sell products to a global audience.

Online survey platforms: Online survey platforms such as Survey Junkie and Swagbucks allow you to earn money by completing surveys and participating in market research studies. This is a simple and easy way to earn money without investing any money.

"The Online Earning Blueprint" is a book that aims to provide readers with a step-by-step guide to building a successful online business. The main points of the book include:

Identifying a profitable niche that aligns with your interests and skills.

Creating high-quality content that provides value to your audience.

Building an engaged and loyal following through social media and email marketing.

Monetizing your online presence through various methods such as affiliate marketing, sponsored content, and e-commerce.

Developing a growth strategy that leverages search engine optimization (SEO) and paid advertising.

Optimizing your website or online platform for maximum conversions and user experience.

Balancing work and personal life and building a sustainable online business.

Overall, the book emphasizes the importance of providing value to your audience and building strong relationships with your followers in order to create a successful and sustainable online business.

Er. Trilok Kumar

trilok kumar

Introducing Trilok Kumar, a certified writer and poet who has been shortlisted for the Top 100 prodigies from across the world. His achievements include being selected as a delegate of the Asia World Model United Nations Virtual Conference, an official participant of 'GWR', 'MBR', and 'WBR', and earning a badge from CertiProf.

Trilok is also a co-author of several books, including Euphoria, Dreams, Wanderlust, Mind Maze, Royal, Poem and Short Stories. His talent as a writer has been recognized by many, including being selected for the India Prime Top 100 Author and Researchers 2022, the Literary Awards 2022 (Young Adult Author of the Year), and the Bharat Bhushan Award 2022.

In addition, Trilok is an accomplished educator, having been nominated for the India Top 100 Educators 2022. He has also achieved 250+ e-certificates during the lockdown period, demonstrating his dedication to learning and personal growth.

Trilok has been selected for various international events, including the Harvard-Youth Change the World Workshop, the Future Leaders Model United Nations in Istanbul, and the Arab Youth International MUN 2022. He has also been selected as an eminent personality for 100 powerful personalities 2022 by Glantor X Media and shortlisted for the Be Star Award 2022.

His remarkable achievements have earned him the National Book of Records Approval and the India Book of Record Holder title. Trilok has been recommended for an Honorary doctorate degree by the India Book of Records for his extraordinary achievements, and has been awarded the राष्ट्रीय रत्न सम्मान- 2022 as the Youngest Writer.

Trilok's incredible journey and achievements are truly inspiring, making him an exceptional role model for aspiring writers and educators. His works are an inspiration for many, and his dedication to excellence continues to inspire others to pursue their dreams with passion and hard work.

9 798889 861447

Printed by Libri Plureos GmbH in Hamburg, Germany